THE GOOD FIGHT

VICTORY IS YOURS

Shareta Green

Scripture quotations marked CJB are from the Complete Jewish Bible

Scripture quotations marked KJV are from the King James Version

Scripture quotations marked NIV are from the New International Version

Cover by Les
ISBN: 978-0-578-68396-6
Contact me: info@goodfightfaith.org

I Timothy 6:12

"Fight the good fight of the faith, take hold of the eternal life to which you were called when you testified so well to your faith before many witnesses."-CJB

TABLE OF CONTENTS

ACKNOWLEDGMENTS

I would like to thank Jesus Christ, my Lord and Savior. He is my best friend and has been a source of hope and strength for me. I thank him for the challenges and heartaches of my past that drew me closer in developing a relationship with him.

I thank The Life Center Church for the opportunity to praise dance, sing, and be trained in the prophetic and make use of my gifts on the teams to pour into the lives of others.

I thank YWAM Houston, TX, for exposing me to evangelism and street outreach with people showing me how to be bold and not be ashamed of the gospel of Jesus Christ.

I thank the people who rejected me, disappointed me, sabotaged me, and mocked me. They pushed me to draw closer to Christ and helped me to become the Godly woman I am today.

I thank the prophetic ministers who have spoken into my life and those who spoke about writing a book, Ike, Cory, and Dr. Bessie.

I thank Elder Dorathy and Dr. Sharon for ministering deliverance and praying for me in times of sickness, emotional wounds, and allowing me to serve on their teams.

I thank Dr. Bessie and Bishop Ludd for trusting the Holy Spirit in me to grace their pulpit, challenging me to speak in front of the congregation with confidence and boldness.

I thank my Mom for being a pillar of strength and support, and my siblings for caring and being an example to others in the body of Christ.

I thank the leadership team at Prayer City Eagles Chapel for welcoming me to pray with them on intercessory prayer nights and praying for me.

INTRODUCTION

Have you ever felt like you were the only one? The only one without a good job, without knowing your purpose, without a good career, good friends, spouse, family, children, good health? You look around and you see people in their nice cars, beautiful homes, and exceptionally fashionable clothes. They are attractive, they travel the world, they seamlessly have little to no cares and they appear to live on easy street. You are experiencing the middle age jitters and reflecting on where you have been, where you are, and where you are going. Trust me and believe that even though you may think this is true, you're NOT the only one.

This book is for those struggling to keep up with life and have been discouraged about ever experiencing or achieving the dreams and goals like others around them. They seem to experience life so seamlessly. You have made your mistakes and have moved on. You keep doing what you can to provide for yourself as an independent man or woman. Yet despite your strides, prayers, and living your life as an example, you wonder about the how, who, and when your breakthrough will happen. You have felt like God does not care despite your efforts and your good works. When you take a few steps forward, the disappointment of others appears to push you back. You want to be in a place where hardships will end. You have asked and been mad at God at times for making you wait. Just know that God has a time and season for everything. We must go through processes in our life to make us stronger and become established as an example and a source of strength for others. God is a rewarder and he wants us to look like him. Consider yourself chosen by him to accomplish a great purpose. The greater the suffering, the pain, the rejection, the disappointment, the wait- the greater you will reign in body, soul, spirit, and mind. This book is to show you that God is your source of everything. It will show you how to stand and win your battles, have hope, and walk in victory with Christ.

Let's talk about some areas that appear troubling, and despite them, how to walk in triumph.

Chapter 1

IDENTITY

1) IDENTITY- Webster's defines identity as "the fact of being who or what a person or thing is." In the world, there are a plethora of sources telling us who we are, where we should live and what we should look like. The media, families, and communities we live in have somewhat given us the image we and others see day to day. Your identity is formed by your own thoughts about yourself and it can be influenced by others' thoughts toward you. The question to ask is what are you portraying and is that really who you are? Consider the clothes you wear, the car you drive, the job you have, the life you live.

Ask yourself, deep down, are you happy or are you just putting on a façade?

We have to determine the source of why we are the way we are. There are family members, co-workers, schoolmates, relatives, and community members that— believe it or not— have shaped our identity. These groups have either said words of blessing: *how can I support you, you are great, you are powerful, you have such an awesome gift, you are beautiful/handsome, you can do it, never give up* or have you heard words of negativity such as *you're ugly, you're not smart, you are just like so and so, you will never make it in life, you have no value.* Proverbs 18:21 says, "Death and life are in the power of the tongue: and they that love it shall eat the fruit thereof."-KJV. Science has researched that what we hear and experience in life will affect our soul. Our internal thoughts, emotions, and perspectives carry into our adult life.

As adults, our identity stems from a childhood filled with dreams, hopes, and expectations and/or trauma that scarred us and it's possible that we have not dealt with painful experiences of the past properly. As adults, people who have heard negative words and seen bad behavior from others normally hold on to that in adulthood becoming angry, bitter, and frustrated displaying a false identity. We have, however, seen there are adults who have taken those negative experiences and become powerful significant people who have made a tremendous impact in people's lives offering hope, and a way toward a better future.

You have tried to obtain a position financially and it seems like you keep getting knocked down. You don't even know who you have become as an adult. Unfavorable life circumstances can bring us into a dark place where you become bitter and people are turned off by your presence. John 10 states God gave us life and life abundantly where we enjoy God, enjoy others and enjoy ourselves. What happens when we lose sight of the identity that God wants us to have? Matthew 22:37 speaks of loving God and loving others. Well, how do you love when you have never been loved in a healthy way?

Genesis 6 states we were born and made in God's image. God is perfect and he loves you so much that John 3:16 tells us Jesus came to die for your sins. When you feel like you are not good enough or have made a mistake, you must repent (turn away from the wrong) and confess and he will forgive you. Thank God he is a forgiving person who loves to forgive.

God does not make "junk;" there is a reason you are here. You are here to make an impact in the life of someone. There is someone out there now that needs to be inspired by the gift/talent that God has given you.

When talking about identity, you want to examine these things

1) Is it healthy?
2) What are you showing others?
3) God's View about you

Health means having a positive physical, mental and emotional state and applies to someone who has no disease, or a reduced risk of disease. Some characteristics that display a healthy identity are:

A. Going to Church, Loving God, Praying, Reading the Bible
B. Serving and helping others
C. Being Kind and Respectful
D. Showcasing your gifts and performing your Best
E. Valuing and Loving yourself

Notice these ideas come from an internal place, not external. Too often, our identity has been formed based on material items and possessions and our identity has been consumed by material objects with temporary satisfaction.

It's the meaningful actions you do in life that really affects the lives of others.

In the Bible, Jesus talks about the Be-Attitudes in Matthew 5: 3-12 and the Fruit of the Spirit in Galatians 5:22-24. Jesus talks about having character and pleasing him. So often, our identity is distorted from the image that God already established for us. We can stray so far from his truth we get lost and become the opposite of his original intent for our lives. People can steer us away from the direction of God and not even realize it.

Some questions to ask and determine: Have you been steered away?

1) Are you supported in the things you love to do and have a passion for?

_____

_____

_____

2) Are people constantly wanting you to follow them instead of you creating your own path?

_____

_____

_____

3) Have you begun an assignment and due to life circumstances put it on the shelf and settled for less instead of receiving the best?

_____

_____

_____

4) Have you lost your joy and enthusiasm for what lies ahead by living in someone else's shadow?

_____

_____

_____

5) Have you just buried your dreams and become negative just thinking about them?

_____

_____

_____

We have to be careful who we allow into our lives and what situations we allow to occur in our lives that can stop God's agenda for us. The last thing we want is to fail in fulfilling his purpose while watching others fulfill theirs.

Of course we do need possessions and resources to continue our daily lives. However, when materialism becomes more overpowering than fulfilling and demonstrating the purpose of God, we have to evaluate the identity we are portraying to others. If answering these questions puts you in a place that is not exciting and you feel hopeless or frustrated, I encourage you to

1) Surround yourself with Godly people
2) Write your vision and speak it into existence
3) Encourage yourself and don't give up
4) What Are You Showing Others?

The definition of show is to manifest, display evidence, demonstrate to reveal outwardly, or make apparent, to allow or cause to be visible, to display or allow to be perceived (a quality, emotion or characteristic).

When people look at you, do they see a person they aspire to become or are they turned off by your attitude and bad behavior? Unfortunately, people are reactive and instead of being proactive, we wear our emotions not only on our sleeves but our arms, head, legs. Just all over. We have bad days and moments where we can come out of our natural everyday self and show our "other side." This "other side," which is negative should be revealed hardly, barely or never. The more we come to know Christ, the less we reveal our natural self and reveal more of the Christ that lies within us.

In Romans 8: 7-10, we read, "The carnal mind is enmity against God: for it is not subject to the law of God, neither indeed can be. So then they that are in the flesh cannot please God. But ye are not in the flesh, but in the Spirit, if so be that the Spirit of God dwell in you. Now if any man have not the Spirit of Christ, he is none of his. And if Christ be in you, the body is dead because of sin; but the Spirit is life because of righteousness."-KJV

We have to realize that consistently walking in our flesh (Galatians 5) is not pleasing God, and if we say we love God and we are his sons and daughters, why do our lives not reflect it? Why do we show more of our flesh and talk more about humanism than the Holy Spirit that lies within those who have been saved by Christ. Who is the Holy Spirit? The Holy Spirit is a teacher, counselor, and helper When your "other side" becomes your M.O. and when people see and think of you in that which is in a negative connotation, we have to reevaluate our inner selves and draw closer to Christ. It can come to where our original self (as referenced in Gen 1:27) has been carried off by the winds and tossed into the sea of forgetfulness. We have to first realize when we are indulging a negative influence and how to stop it.

We don't want to displease God with our continual carnal behavior.

1) If you explode every blue moon or red moon, it's okay, don't feel like you are a bad person. You want to recognize when you are getting angry. James 5:16 says, "Therefore confess your sins to each other and pray for each other so that you may be healed. The prayer of a righteous person is powerful and effective." –NIV

It reminds us to recognize what has transpired over the past few days, weeks, months and years recognizing our triggers.

Solution: Stop at that moment, pray and ask God for his forgiveness

2) If you have been operating negatively in a particular area for days, weeks, months, and years:

You must take an examination and seek and fast for the root of the issue and when the problem began.

I've noticed that kids are ambitious, optimistic and are exploratory in every way. Even when I was a child, I had no cares, worries and everything would be provided for me. I never let what others said about me matter. As I grew older, the opinions of others overshadowed the existence of who God made me to be and their voices became louder than the truth about myself. This is common with many people. Some people have received positive words of affirmation as they grew older and some, unfortunately, have not. To stay grounded and keep out the negative external voices we must have a relationship with Christ. Christ sent the Holy Spirit to comfort us, direct us, and teach us the way we should go. Our direction in life is directly affected by who we surround ourselves with and who we listen to.

In the book of Genesis, God told Adam and Eve not to eat of the tree of good and evil. They were living a perfect life. Everything was handed to them on a platter. They may have experienced love, laughter, and had everything at their disposal. In the book of Psalms 1:1, it says "Blessed is the man that walketh not in the counsel of the ungodly, nor standeth in the way of sinners, nor sitteth in the seat of the scornful. 2 But his delight is in the law of the LORD; and in his law doth he meditate day and night." -KJV

Adam and Eve were assigned to serve God and love one another and take care of the land. Genesis 3:1 talks about how the serpent came and questioned Eve. He asked, "Did God really say not to eat of the tree. The voice of the serpent became louder than God's voice and they had to leave the Garden of Eden.

Who is speaking into your life? If they are speaking into your life, what are they saying? Are your inner voices and other voices pulling you into the presence of God or pulling you away? Yes, sometimes things just happen and there are situations that bad circumstances or events happen because God wants to refine us in this fire.

Here are some questions to ponder:

Who is speaking into your life and what are they suggesting you do?

_____

_____

_____

Do you feel at peace or are your frustrated when you are around that person(s)?

_____

_____

_____

Does the conversation always appear to be what's in the best interest of them?

_____

_____

_____

If you have answered these questions and are not satisfied: Here are some solutions:

(1) Remove yourself from negative and unproductive people and activities. Pray, fast, seek godly counsel, attend healing and deliverance session(s), surround yourself with Godly people, and of course, be in a good church home.

(2) Declare God's Word over your life: I am an example, I crucify my flesh, I forgive others and God forgives me, I am loved and can show love, and I can walk alone and follow God's plans.

(3) God's View

Jeremiah 29:11 tells us, "I know the plans I have for you, declares the Lord, plans to prosper you and not to harm you, plans to give you a hope and future."-NIV

When we come into this world, we are the joy in the eyes of those who love us. We receive a lot of attention, but somewhere along the way, as we grew older, we no longer were the center of attention and what was cute about us became problematic. In the previous section, we talked about identity and how we need to have our identity in Christ. Our teenage years are probably one of the best and/or worst times of our lives, and our successful negotiating of these crucial years depended on the support we did or did not receive from family, peers, church, and community. My childhood years were more encouraging and supportive than my teenage years. During my childhood years, I had true friends, family support, and enjoyed life with no cares or concerns and I was received for who I was not for who someone wanted me to be. I didn't know what it meant to feel different or unaccepted regarding the way I looked or the color of my skin.

Our teenage years is when we lose our individualism from childhood and take on false identities under the influence of others. Others put peer pressure on us, stressing what we should look like, how to dress, who to hang out with, what clubs to join, whose party you should attend, where to sit in the cafeteria, and what car to drive. The more we allow someone else to alter our lifestyle, the less unique we become and we can negatively transform into a copy of someone else's original. We carry these characteristics into our adulthood, attempting to conform to the liking of someone else to get attention. Often, people label us using the term "sellout," defined as "a person who compromises his or her personal values, integrity, talent or the like, for money or personal advancement." As adults, some people have jobs they do for fame, finance, notoriety, and some work because they have a passion and love for what they do. If you asked adults in the employment field if they working in an area of their choice, most will say no. Deloitte Center for Edge Today documented that only 13 percent of people love their jobs.

What happens to the dream when we were kids of becoming a pilot, a teacher, writer, singer, dancer, doctor, or engineer? What is the dream you loved so much! As we get older, the thought may be in our mind to pursue something else, but we settle for what we can get versus finding where our passion lies. God is the one who put dreams inside of us before we were born. Life, circumstances, hopelessness, rejection are just a few factors that bring us from our place of "I know I can" to "I think I can." Don't worry if you are in this place, you are NOT alone. There are dreams and visions that the Lord gives us and there is a process we must go through to achieve those goals. Nothing that the Lord shows us happens overnight and there is a process. The challenge is keeping the "I know I can" despite the obstacles and challenges that come our way. How many of you are in the "I think I can" or the "I know I can" category. Life has gotten its best of you and rejection has taken its course where you have accepted defeat and failure.

God gave many people in the Bible the end promise but their situation was opposite of where they ultimately desired to be. How many of you feel the same way? Are you looking at everyone else with plentiful finances, family, good health, dreams, homes, and cars? God's view of obtaining the promises he has for us will be a journey but the reward will be greater than the struggle. The key is to keep going and to never give up. If you give up, the enemy wins, but if you stay in the race to see what the end will be, God wins.

In I Samuel 16: 13, David was anointed by the Prophet Samuel to be King and in 2 Samuel 5:4, David actually became King. There was a process of servanthood, battling, becoming homeless, leading an army, writing songs of love and pain to God, and losing loved ones. He went through many experiences. David is one example that demonstrates the ability to fight and stand on God's word. When he was anointed, none of his journey was revealed to him upfront.

When we become servants, sons and daughters, often God will not tell us about the process. At times, things will become worse before they become better and it is in the "process phase" where we are truly tested whether we trust God and hold on to his word or not. Or it's in this phase where we will become discouraged and change his course to walk in our own. In 2 Corinthians 1:20, "For as many are the promises of God, in him are the Yes, and in him the Amen, unto the glory of God by us".-KJV. And Isaiah 55:11 says "So shall my word be that goeth forth out of my mouth: it shall not return unto me void, but it shall accomplish that which I please, and it shall prosper in the thing whereto I sent it."-KJV

Here are some things to think about:

What were your childhood dreams?

_____

_____

_____

What or who has blocked you from obtaining those dreams?

_____

_____

_____

What are activities you do for fun and what do you like or dislike about your job?

_____

_____

_____

Ways to get back on track toward your promise:

* Surround yourself with like-minded people.
* Make an effort every day to step toward your goals.
* Find a person that will hold you accountable.

Chapter 2

RELATIONSHIPS (OR THE LACK THEREOF)

elationship defined by Oxford dictionary is "the way in which two or more concepts, objects, or people are connected, or the state of being connected; the state of being connected by blood or marriage; the way in which two or more people or groups regard and behave toward each other."

When talking about relationships, I would like to focus on

1) Self

2) Socializing

3) God

1) SELF

You may ask how you can be in a relationship with yourself. Well, it correlates back to the discussion on identity. Who did God create you to be in his image? It's NOT the image of man. Philosophers understood this meaning "know thyself" and its importance. Understanding who you are allows you to examine areas of weaknesses and strengths and how you are presenting yourself to others. With weaknesses, it's important to understand your triggers, what makes you mad, happy, sad, and glad. What motivates you in life? What holds you back from achieving your goals? Knowing yourself allows you to keep your moods in balance and keeps you from exploding in times of chaos and stressful situations. I'm sure you can think of situations where you reacted in a manner that had resulted in a harmful or negative consequence. Knowing yourself can prevent or reduce negative outcomes that may not have happened if you controlled your thoughts and emotions, not letting external triggers light a fire of anger and frustration to manifest. How often did you lose the promotion because you were late to work, argued with a co-worker, got upset at a customer? How many people are knowledgeable but can't lead others because they lie, have filthy mouths, and have bad character and unethical practices? How many people's relationships are weak due to their being selfish, not communicating, and trying to control others? The goal is to recognize areas of weakness and admit them. If you are in denial about areas damaging to yourself and others, then there will be struggles accomplishing all your goals because others will see the flaws within you. There has to come a time where "knowing thyself" takes precedence over wanting to be wrong or right. We must learn to stop controlling the situation and making excuses for not wanting to be a better person in society.

No one is perfect, we all have made mistakes. The question is are we learning from those mistakes? In the bible, David became king. However, he had a problem with lust and it resulted in the murder of a man. Samson was a Nazarite who was to be devoted to the Lord and he married a Philistine woman and not an Israelite as was the law. This resulted in him losing his strength to fight his enemies. Our mistakes land us in problematic places and we will suffer the consequences for our decisions. But with repentance and the mercy of God, there is always a way out.

Romans 3:23 tells us, "All have sinned and come short of the Glory of God."-KJV

James 5:16, we are told, "Confess your faults one to another, and pray one for another, that ye may be healed. The effectual fervent prayer of a righteous man availeth much."-KJV.

I Corinthians 11:28 reads, "But let a man examine himself, and so let him eat of the bread and drink of the cup."-KJV

James 1:19 "My dear brothers and sisters, take note of this: Everyone should be quick to listen, slow to speak and slow to become angry."-NIV

Let's examine some weakness and steps to overcome them:

What makes you upset?

_____

_____

_____

Who makes you upset?

_____

_____

_____

What happens when things don't your way?

_____

_____

_____

How do you handle stress?

_____

_____

_____

Steps to overcome weaknesses
   1) Confess them
   2) Stop and Think, Then Act Positively
   3) Pray and ask for advice from Godly people
   4) Remove yourself from the situation
   5) Celebrate when you do well

Knowing yourself is beneficial not only in identifying your weaknesses but also your strengths. Knowing and identifying your weaknesses helps you grow and mature, however knowing your strengths allows you to be confident and strive in areas of comfort and familiarity. God gives us talents (earned because of training to refine and perfect; and an inheritance) and gifts (given to you or a natural ability) to be a blessing and an inspiration to others and help them grow in their areas of weakness they may be encouraged and strengthened.

The areas of strength gives us the ability to obtain employment that our employer may capitalize on our skills so we may earn promotions, train others, and become entrepreneurs. When you operate in an area of strength, you are not only confident, but others will see the confidence and will seek you out for mentorship and training opportunities. When you are aware of where your confidence lies and how you can succeed, then life has purpose and you realize there is something you have to offer.

Whether you are a dancer, cook, singer, coach, teacher, administrator, athlete, programmer, doctor and the list goes on . . . people need you. The question becomes not just are you skilled in certain areas but how are you presenting yourself before others? In business, to make money, you must supply customers with products or services that will meet their needs also providing them with an experience they will remember. Sometimes the item may not be of the best quality, however since the customer service was outstanding, they would come back. There are places I will not visit due to the lack of positive customer service, regardless of the product. Realize that your talent or gift must transcend the philosophy of just obtaining a customer. To continue and remain strongly supported, you must retain customers by giving back and showing appreciation.

What are some ways you can share your talents and gifts with others?

1) Giving back: A way to show others where your strengths lie is volunteering your services for free to community organizations, churches, schools, talent shows and more.

2) Availability: When you have an opportunity to join a group of people or attend an event where you can showcase who you are, you can add value and benefit to peoples' lives.

3) Training Others: There is something about you that others should want to learn from. What area(s) are you proficient in and what methods have you discovered that can help others in their journey to build confidence, develop their life skills, and become entrepreneurial.

Some of you may be asking, what am I good at? What is it about me that people will seek me out for? You may be a person who is good at performing and accomplishing a task making others look good, however, you are left with nothing to show for all you have done for others. Increasing their bonuses, raising their profitable metrics, bringing in customers, and you don't even get a thank you. Regardless, we need to learn how to honor our superiors and perform at our best with the correct attitude. This behavior is pleasing to the Lord and helps you to remain humble and have Godly character. I'm sure there has come a point where you have to ask the question. Is this ALL that life has to offer me? There is something I can do that I enjoy with a passion that will inspire me to be eager and ready to wake up and get going every morning.

Let's examine how you can move from being an employee to becoming and employer:

1) Write down what you are good at.

_____

_____

_____

2) What group or organizations can you join where others have a similar passion?

_____

_____

_____

3) Refine and Perfect your gift, and practice getting better every day. List what you will do daily or weekly towards becoming better.

Monday_____

_____

Tuesday_____

_____

Wednesday_____

_____

Thursday_____

_____

Friday_____

_____

Saturday_____

_____

Sunday_____

_____

SOCIAL LIFE

"Social" is defined by Westers Dictionary as "of or relating to human society, the interaction of the individual and the group, or the welfare of human beings as members of society, tending to form cooperative and interdependent relationships with others."

We live in a world where we intermingle with one another whether our interactions are positive or negative. Our positive interactions help us emotionally with our physical health and outlook on life. When we have loving people in our lives, they will not only impact us to move forward coaching us, and encouraging us; they will also challenge us to become better. *Harvard Health* wrote an article, "*The health benefits of strong relationships.*" The article stated that social relationships allow us to exchange ideas, lend social support to one another, check-in with one another, and influence our long-term health. Health includes adequate sleep, a good diet, and no excesses such as smoking or drinking. People with a good social life are happier, have fewer health problems and live longer. Social activities improve our overall health, build up our immune function, relieve stress levels, help gut function, and insulin regulation. It's interesting how having a strong network will bring so much joy and happiness. However, how do we get to where relationships are a necessity, not an option? It has been proven that our social networks impact our outlook on life, our pursuits, and health. Why is it there are people who deny the importance of socializing?

People have been scarred from their childhood and bring those scars into adulthood with empty promises and they develop mistrust for people and what they have to offer. This causes people to live a life of isolation interacting only when necessary. Not that being independent will not cause you to succeed in life, but it may not allow you to advance as far with your goals. Independence has its benefits, of course, such as paying bills, preparing meals, budgeting and finance, self-development, boosting confidence, self-reliance, and a personal sense of freedom and accomplishment. Yes, there are benefits to independence. However, we should focus more on being inter-dependent. Inter-dependence informs us we need each other. We do not live on an island alone nor should we be totally dependent, relying on others for our overall decisions and well-being. Personally, I lived in the independent stage for 15+ years and not until the last few years did I realize that people are necessary for my life to be happy, fulfilling, and productive. The independent stage may sound rewarding and several medals of honor should be awarded, however, there were so many struggles with trusting others, financial stability, and loneliness I would not recommend complete independence as a permanent way of life.

Some people cringe when it comes to social connections and mingling with others. The thinking process begins in your teenage years and transcends into adulthood. The *Greater Good Berkeley Magazine* had a discussion comparing the quantity vs. quality of the relationship and its meaning for different age groups. The article defines loneliness as "perceived social isolation," the keyword being *perceived*. If two people have the same number of friends, with whom they spend the same amount of time and talk about the same things, one could feel perfectly content while the other could feel lonely." The article showed that the younger the age group, the number of friends was more important, whereas as they grew older, the quality of friendships was more important. It was noted until the age of 7 it was just important to have friends to play games with and have fun. Whereas, in the teenage years, having a peer friend is more critical along with acceptance, and feeling a sense of belonging important for personal self-development. As people head into their 20s, there is a sense of romance and a need for validation, intimacy, and close friendship. Those who were between 30-65 were in the loneliness age group where they had no confidants and no one to share experiences with, regardless of the number of people they encountered.

As an educator, I see this all the time when young people are defined by the number of friends they have, how many parties they are invited to, and how popular they are in school. This belief is a misconception that the number of friends you have determines your status quo, when, in reality, the higher the quantity, the more insecure young people are about themselves. Instead of them pulling their confidence from within, they feed off of the affirmation of others to promote them into a place of excellence, admiration, or popularity. This is an age where appearances, connections, and ambitions override their positive characteristics and they can become conceited, rude, and self-centered.

It's amazing that with the transition into your 20s, the quantity changes and the focus becomes more on career advancement, nurturing relationships, financial stability, marriage, and family obligations. This may not *all* occur in your 20s; however, for most, these changes are ideal but may not reach some of these goals until their 30s. In your 30s, you compare yourself with your high school classmates, neighbors, co-workers, other family members, and ponder on where your time has gone and why you feel behind the eight ball. I am not speaking from just viewing these circumstances but I have experienced these myself. Most of these "American Dream" possibilities were challenging for me to meet those goals and in my 20s and 30s and I did not reach them all. I received my education, I serve society and lived a wholesome "good woman" life, so what happened? I didn't understand the power of connection. I thought it was an option and became superwoman for 15+ years. It wasn't until my later years in my 30s that I realized connection is not an option; it is mandatory if you want to succeed in life, not just maintain at one level. Lay down your Pride and let someone know, I need you!

Here are some tips and suggestions to help you push past social isolation:

1) Get rid of your independent mindset. Realize you need people. Find a group of people that do the same things you enjoy or have interest in, and join it.

2) Take the first step. So often, we wait on people to promote us, push us, grow us, and mentor us. Be the person you want someone to be for you. Whatever talent or gift you have, find how you can help by volunteering yourself.

3) Join a Church. You need a spiritual advisor to give you direction and advice so as you advance and become a person of wisdom, strength, and godly character

Genesis 2:18 presents an idea that encourages connections: The LORD God said, "It is not good

for the man to be alone. I will make a helper suitable for him."-NIV

And Psalms 1:1 tells us, "Blessed is the one who does not walk in step with the wicked or stand in the way that sinners take or sit in the company of mockers" -NIV

Matthew 18:20 reads, "For where two or three gather in my name, there am I with them" –NIV

Reflect on these questions

1) Where are you holding back from others?

_____

_____

_____

_____

_____

_____

_____

2) Name 3 things you could show someone how to do today? Do it within 30 days

_____

_____

_____

_____

_____

_____

_____

3) List groups in your areas of similar interest. Find a Meetup Group Today

_____

_____

_____

_____

_____

_____

_____

_____

_____

_____

_____

_____

_____

_____

_____

Chapter 3

HEALTH

ealth: The definition of Health as defined by Word Central is "the condition of being sound in body, mind, and spirit; freedom from disease, the overall condition of the body; flourishing condition; a toast to someone's health or success."

Our health is a topic of discussion not often on the minds of people until something happens, and then we reflect over the past few days, months, and years on how we have been treating our body. The healthcare industry in

America has spent billions of dollars on visits, exams, imaging, treatments and prescriptions. The food options in America are quite extensive compared to other countries, yet these options have contributed to a lot of health problems in our country. There are preservatives, additives, oils, artificial sugars, and more that the Federal Drug Administration (FDA) allows in our products, which can have negative side effects in the long term. *FoodBabe* is an article that describes the differences between the US and the UK and its ingredients used for similar products. For example, McDonald's French Fries in the UK does not use hydrogenated oils; Mountain Dew and Heinz Ketchup has no High Fructose Corn Syrup; and Doritos has no artificial coloring. The UK found a way to market and sell these products to customers without the harmful ingredients that the US puts in our foods. High Fructose Corn Syrup can lead to diabetes; artificial coloring can contribute to allergies and hyperactivity; hydrogenated oil, also known as Tran's fats, can lead to heart health issues. These hidden ingredients are listed on the products, however, research on what's in our foods must be left up to the consumer. A few years back, the FDA required that packaged food companies give warnings if their foods contain "partially hydrogenated oils." But this information is only beneficial if the consumer cares about their health. If the UK can find alternative sources to replace harmful ingredients, why can't the US do the same? These are just some food concerns that affect our health, but there are also drugs, alcohol, stress, diseases, and sanitary conditions that will affect our health as well.

Our mindset on health is important as this is where our thoughts come from and how we project life. It's important to know there is a brain-mind connection. The brain is the tangible physical substance that receives input from our mind. The mind tells the brain what to do and it carries out those thoughts and signals throughout our body. These signals eventually will be transmitted into our cells and our cells will react based on our thoughts. The reaction can be positive or negative, depending on what we think, say, or what we allow to impact our lives. The power of words is very influential concerning our direction in life. The words we use, whether negative or positive, will steer you in a direction of empowerment or stagnation. Regardless of our family circumstances, school teachers, community stakeholders, we individually have to decide for our own lives and where we want to see ourselves in 3, 5, 10 years. Our mindset must not be on what we don't have or what we can't do, but on our goals and who can help us reach them. Yes, there are people who seem to have everything handed to them on a platter and they get whatever they ask for, and then there are those who don't even know what a dream is, or how to get out their situation. Regardless, goals can be met! For some, it may be the lack of finances and/or the lack of support to obtain their goals and it may take longer. The saying goes, "it's better to try and fail than not to try at all."

Some people will fail. You want to succeed, then you must be part of the process, everyone can and will make mistakes. People get stressed out, frustrated, angry, and maybe even have fits of rage because of time, situations, and circumstances. Health can be affected eventually and going back to the relationship discussion, remember, having positive people around you can reduce or alleviate preventable health situations.

At seven, I had a small vitiligo spot on my chin and inside my elbow, which remains to this day. I am not sure why it happened; however, it did not affect my mindset or activities playing with other children. Had I been out-casted or made to feel shameful and rejected, my childhood experience might have been negative and lonely. After college graduation, I was stressed when looking for a job, a career that would pay me a bachelor's salary so I could drive a nice car and live in a nice house. When I was living in public housing and driving a 1990 Ford Taurus. I ended up substitute teaching, which was a very stressful job, and after so many years, my health was affected by worry. I was not in a relationship to support my overall well-being, and I saw a skin rash on my fingers and elbows known as eczema. The rash comes and goes based on my outlook and perception on life. The more positive thoughts I have about myself, the stronger the community of people that speak into my life, and my growing relationship with Christ are all factors that reduce my stress levels improving my health.

Our spiritual health is very important. When we go through life putting our trust in ourselves and others without relying on God to give us power to overcome, we will only go so far in our human strength. No matter how physically or mentally capable you are, you must rely on the power of Christ to uplift you, empower you, and heal you from wounds and failures. The Holy Spirit was released when Christ was resurrected. Holy Spirit's function directs, teaches, and guides us in our daily everyday activities giving us hope, wisdom, and peace to carry on. There will be trials and tribulations, blockages, hindrances, failures, mistakes, losses and gains, and you have to rely not on man's strength but on the strength of the Holy Spirit to get you through every situation.

It's interesting to know that when tough times hit, people become spiritual. This is because they know they need a supernatural intervention beyond their control. The challenge for some is to understand God does not want you to call on him only in hard times, but in good times as well. He is available for those who are in relationship with him and is only a prayer away. Prayer is the first thing people do when they're desperate and it is essential for every believer to stay connected and receive answers, not just for ourselves but for others as well. Why do we put God in the back seat and turn to Him as the last resort when he supersedes the mind of man, and his intelligence transcends our imagination. Are we distracted by jobs, family, kids, life, TV and social media? We have to take an examination of our priorities. The thing we care for the most is where we invest most of our time. Our relationship with Christ, pleasing him, and following his ways should be our first priority.

Matthew's gospel 6:33 says, "But seek first his kingdom and his righteousness, and all these things will be given to you as well." -NIV

I Corinthians 3:19 claims, "For the wisdom of this world is foolishness in God's sight. As it is written: "He catches the wise in their craftiness." -NIV

Isaiah 55:6 asserts, "Seek the LORD while he may be found; call on him while he is near. -NIV

Psalms 46:1 reminds us, "God is our refuge and strength, a very present help in trouble."-KJV

And III John 1:2 points out, "Dear friend, I pray that you may enjoy good health and that all may go well with you, even as your soul is getting along well." -NIV

Here are some tips on getting better with your health:

1) Master your emotions - Many times our personal situations cause us to become angry and upset with people without justification or the slightest disturbance will cause us to become upset. Note the consequences of your actions and the impact they have on others. Most importantly, the Bible tells us to examine ourselves; realize that God sees everything and we want to please him. Think before you act

2) Value what you eat - Food that is better for you may be more expensive. However, you must get back to preparing your own foods and cut back on buying package foods. Read the labels and the ingredients before you purchase. Take time to research the ingredients and its positive or negative effects on your body. We only get one body and if you want to achieve your goals do your best to keep it healthy. Also exercise once, twice or three times per week.

3) Seek a Relationship with God - Many times, we don't feel as if we need God, but we often wait until times get tough. It's imperative you find a church home that can help you grow and develop your relationship with God. When times get tough, you will learn to become stronger as well as how to handle situations, reducing your stress and episodes of anger and frustration.

Here are some questions to ask.

What does your diet consist of and how do you feel after you eat?

_____

_____

_____

_____

How often do you exercise?

_____

_____

_____

_____

What do you do when you get upset? What are some positive outlets to prevent an explosion?

_____

_____

_____

_____

Do you receive Godly Advice? Who can you call when in need?

_____

_____

_____

_____

Chapter 4

PURPOSE

*"**Purpose**" as defined by dictionary.com is "the reason for which something exists or is done, made, used, an intended or desired result, end, aim, goal, determination, resoluteness."*

We all are here for a reason. It's unfortunate there are people, especially our teenagers, who because of social isolation, abuse, and unsafe family environments, commit suicide. According to *PBS News Hour*, the level of young adults and teens committing suicide has reached its highest mark in the last

20 years. Between the ages of 15 to 24, suicide ranked as the 2nd most leading cause of death. Close to 6,500 people in 2017 among that age group committed suicide, trailing the 1st place cause of death, car accidents. Research was done on some underlying probable causes, which were opioid use and social media.

Peer pressure is an overwhelming problem not just among teenagers, but among young adults as well. Teenagers battle with identity, health factors, drug use, school engagement, fashion, dating, social media, bullying and making friends. Adult peer pressure includes jobs, career, family, promotion, personal pressures, obligations, and how to live a successful life. With these factors falling short or unmet, discouragement, depression, hopelessness, and defeat settles in, which can lead to suicide.

People encounter all of these pressures on a daily basis. Knowing your purpose can filter out the trash the world implants in your mind and help you stay focused on your God-given assignment. Some of these battles are self-inflicted, meaning we magnify these problems and participate in them rather than push them away. One person's purpose may be different from the other. Society has framed what "the American Dream" is and if people cannot fit within that frame, then they become stressed out and worry if they will ever achieve its goals and dreams. Yes, we should have something to strive for in life. However, so many of us are trying to fit a round peg into a square hole. We each have a path and it's time to finds yours.

How to find your purpose making sure your round peg fits into a round hole. You first must realize that you do have a purpose, and there *is* a reason you are here. Most people have to think, ponder, reflect, or inquire from others about why they were born and how they can affect the earth. Without the realization of your purpose, you may never know why you exist. You may just think you're taking up time and space. Your purpose is identified by something God has given you, a gift or talent which you are to use to bless others.

To identify your purpose:

1) Write down what makes you smile?

_____

_____

_____

_____

_____

_____

2) What do you want to show/teach people what you can do?

_____

_____

_____

_____

_____

_____

3) If you had to create something what would it be?

_____

_____

_____

_____

_____

_____

You may have a list of several ideas but narrow it down to the top 3 most important thoughts and reflect on those. For example, you like cooking, and you would love to show people how to cook using fresh foods and spices. You would love to find a way to mix spices that are mild and flavorful, yet not too spicy. With this in mind you can surround yourself with people in related careers. Find someone locally or nationally and subscribe to their social media page or put yourself on his or her email list. Look up internships or work opportunities as a teenager or college student to gain experience in those fields building up your résumé experience. Challenge yourself to step toward one goal and move forward. Don't compare yourself to other people or worry about how fast they are going or the resources they have. Step out in the unknown and in moving then blessings and opportunity will meet you along the way.

It's important to note that even though you have an objective, there will be naysayers, people who will distract you and challenge you to get you off course. There will be financial institutions, funding, business plans that will shut down and will reject you along the way. Failure is inevitable and is a part of life. It's not that challenges won't come; it's how you handle them along the way. It's important to know that you need to have those positive social relationships to keep pushing you toward your mark. Positive affirmation will outweigh negativity anytime, anywhere, and anyplace.

In the Book of Nehemiah, Sanballat and Tobiah were attempting to distract Nehemiah from rebuilding the walls and were sending messages to him, trying to get him to stop. Nehemiah knew the order from God and was given permission by the King to go back and rebuild. When you are aware of your Godly assignment, the enemy will come in to stop, block, or slow down progress. His objective doesn't want you to reach your goals.

Deuteronomy 20:4 states: "For the Lord your God is the one who goes with you to fight for you against your enemies to give you victory." -NIV

Philippians 3:14 says, "I press toward the high mark for the prize of the high calling of God in Christ Jesus" -KJV

Ephesians 1:11 tells us, "In him we were also chosen, having been predestined according to the plan of him who works out everything in conformity with the purpose of his will"-NIV

You have to take an examination of your circle. Who is around you and what are they saying about you? Are they helping you become a better person or are they luring you away to satisfy their own means. You have to take advantage of your own life and consider where you can see yourself in a few years. If you have to cut people out of your life or pull away from them, then do so graciously. The goal is not to lock yourself in a room or hide in a cabin. The objective is to evaluate your purpose and who can support you while you are on this journey.

Chapter 5

REJECTION

"Rejection" is defined by Cambridge Dictionary as "the act of refusing to accept, use, or believe someone or something; the act of not giving someone the love and attention they want and expect; the act of refusing to accept an idea, suggestion, or proposal."

News flash! At some point in our lives, everyone has been rejected; young, middle age, or old. It's a part of our lives and happens with our family members, strangers, co-workers, bosses, teammates, community groups, children, and the list goes on.

Depending on the person and depending on the person's standards and or beliefs, what one person finds offensive may not be offensive to another. For example, one day a person was burping out loud in a grocery store near the vegetables. A different shopper told management and management politely addressed the potential customer. They asked the customer to be mindful of where they are burping and if they could move away from the fresh foods. That person may have felt rejected by the store and may never come back, another may brush off the incident and come back the next day. Again, much of how we perceive rejection is based on our thoughts, our ideals, and self-perception. In another example, a young girl just started ballet and she could not jump as high, stretch as easily, or balance herself on the beam as gracefully as the other students. Other ballet participants may be more seasoned and have an easier time accomplishing the basic tasks, and they bully the young girl. This behavior makes the young girl reject herself not only from ballet class, but also because she is struggling with the general sense of rejection from her peers. I'm sure there are many situations from your childhood where you felt rejected. Rejection is a part of life. However, when we use rejection to establish our future projections, it can prevent us from moving forward and embracing new possibilities. How many negative memories are we subconsciously holding onto from our childhood, teenage, and young adult years, that negatively affect how we relate with others and pursue opportunities of interest?

Let unmask our rejections and uncover what's holding us back:

1) Name some incidents where you experienced rejection from your childhood.

_____

_____

_____

_____

_____

_____

_____

_____

_____

_____

_____

2) Describe some feelings of rejection during your teenage years.

_____

_____

_____

_____

_____

_____

_____

_____

_____

_____

_____

_____

_____

_____

3) List some rejections you experienced from your family members.

_____

_____

_____

_____

_____

_____

_____

_____

_____

_____

Once you have these lists, take some time to reflect on those situations and memories. Is there anything in your past or current situations where you are still harboring negativity from these rejections? What situations, even just to remember right now, makes you upset? These are areas of rejection you are still holding onto. Take examination and reflect. How have these past encounters defined who you are today? Are there other people who have suffered because of your past? Are there places you have not gone and things you have not done because of the fear of rejection? Take 30 minutes to write and reflect on these questions?

_____

_____

_____

_____

_____

_____

_____

_____

_____

_____

_____

_____

One thing I want you to realize is you are not the only one who has experienced rejection. It's definitely not something anyone wants to experience in life and some people experience rejection in some areas of their life longer than others. Also, we want to make sure that whatever stage of life we are in, and whatever we may encounter, that we don't stay in a place of rejection because we will become stagnant and stop our progression toward our goals. I believe that nothing just happens in life without a reason. Each moment, each incident is there for us to learn, and grow in. Of course, at the time of injury to our self-esteem, we are not thinking ahead but focusing instead on the pain we are experiencing. Something I have learned is that resistance makes you stronger. During many years I've had to grow tough skin and, at the same time, still care and be receptive to others. The Bible gives us many great examples of people who were rejected but were later promoted to powerful positions.

In Genesis, Joseph was despised by his brothers, throwing him into a pit and wanting to sell him off. He was discovered and went to live in Potiphar's house, then was thrown in prison for resisting temptation, yet still used his gifts to prophesy to other people. It wasn't until 13 years later that he was finally recognized for his gifts and became the 2nd in command over Egypt.

In the Book Samuel-David was rejected by his own family. He took care of the sheep, however, he was also noted to be a fighter and played music. He played music to relax King Saul, fought lions, bears, and a giant named Goliath. He was awarded a place to stay, a wife, and a best friend. The king became jealous and wanted to kill David. David was running for his life, became homeless, built an army and fought against his own Israelite people to save his life. He was anointed to be King but he didn't have the full blueprint and it took many years after his rejection before he finally became King.

Jesus experienced the most ultimate rejection, even from his own disciples who denied knowing him. He was ridiculed, mocked, beaten, and falsely accused, however, he still remained obedient to God and remained humble before men. Jesus died on the cross for ALL of our sins and if anything happens in our lives there is nothing that he cannot handle. We can bring all of our sins, problems and circumstances to him. No matter what God does, He does not want us to complain or murmur about anything. There is ALWAYS something to be thankful for and there is always someone worse off than you. To be successful in reaching your goal, on the road from problems to power, we must endure and triumph over life's obstacles. We should continue to respect, love, and honor others, despite how we feel about them.

Best ways to handle rejection:
   (1) Build your self-confidence
   (2) Study God's Word on purpose
   (3) Surround yourself with positive people
   (4) Realize some rejection is always, unfortunately, and inevitable.

Isaiah 53:3 says, "He was despised and rejected by mankind, a man of suffering, and familiar with pain. Like one from whom people hide their faces he was despised, and we held him in low esteem" -NIV

Psalms 27: 6 states, "So I will triumph over my enemies around me. With shouts of joy I will offer sacrifices in His Temple; I will sing, I will praise the Lord.-KJV

Peter 2:17 tells us, "Show proper respect to everyone, love the family of believers, fear God, honor the emperor." -NIV

John 16:33 asserts, "I have told you these things, so that in me you may have peace. In this world you will have trouble. But take heart! I have overcome the world." -NIV

Last, Romans 12:19 simply warns, "Do not take revenge, my dear friends, but leave room for God's wrath, for it is written: "It is mine to avenge; I will repay," says the Lord.- NIV

Chapter 6

FORGIVE YOURSELF

orgiveness is a hard thing. However, it is one of the most important requirements for a Christian believer. If the enemy can prohibit forgiveness to others, it causes blockages and hindrances in our own lives. It's so easy to point fingers at everyone else that we forget we may have had a part to play. No one is perfect. Yes, sometimes, we can truly be innocent, especially with abuse, bullying, and being denied promotion. We often are our own worst critic. Occasions occur in our lives where we find it difficult to forgive someone, such as:

1) Cheating in a relationship

2) Losing trust in Friendship/Family/Educators/Leaders

3) Sexual Abuse/Neglect

4) Peer Bullying

5) Broken Promises

Everyone has fallen into at least one category, regardless of age. At every stage of our lives we may experience different incidents where problems cause us to not forgive. Take some time and reflect on each area and determine where you may be holding un-forgiveness in your heart. These are just some examples, any category not listed please list them here:

_____

_____

_____

_____

_____

_____

_____

_____

Now for each category write down the name of the person(s), what he/she did, when it happened, and how you felt about it.

_____

_____

_____

_____

_____

_____

_____

_____

_____

_____

_____

_____

_____

_____

Now look back into each category and ask yourself was there anything YOU did in the situation that contributed to the problem? Write about that.

_____

_____

_____

_____

_____

_____

_____

_____

_____

_____

_____

_____

_____

_____

The main component for healing unforgiveness- is to forgive. The thing that is the most difficult to do is the thing we need to do, let it go, receive our peace, and move on with our life. To forgive is a healthy choice because it is your own heart you are harming if you let unforgiveness fester. If the person(s) is available by mail, in person, or social media, supported by a loved one or Christian leader, attempt to contact them to forgive them. If they have passed away or you cannot reach them, still forgive them confessing your forgiveness to God. Some have stated that forgiveness is not so much to help them as it is to help yourself. You probably have restless thoughts and maybe even nights still thinking about what happened and they have moved on with their lives without giving the incident or you a thought. But it's time for you to walk in peace and live an abundant life, not one that keeps you trapped by your past.

It is truly one way you can be set free and be delivered and that your blessings from God can be released. You are holding up your own blessings by not forgiving. As long as you remain angry, upset and justify your reason to remain angry, the enemy wins over you. If you release them to God, you gain life.

Here is a prayer to help you with forgiving:

Father, I thank you for your Son Jesus Christ who came to die for me on the cross. Jesus died that I would live a life that is acceptable and pleasing to you. Christ, you died and took every pain I have ever felt and you said that I can give every yoke to you. Un-forgiveness has been tormenting my life and I have problems advancing in jobs, walking in divine health, having positive relationships, launching my business, raising my kids, completing school, not having enough financially, getting along with others, being easily angered and frustrated and not having peace. God, you fashioned me and formed me in your image and I am to reflect you in your image and live according to your ways. I have not been pleasing in your sight by blaming others, and I choose this day to forgive all the people (name them) who harmed me and I ask God that you would forgive me. For your word says if I don't forgive, then I won't be forgiven, and I reap what I sow. I have not been sowing the right things; therefore, I have not been reaping the right things. I choose this day to forgive others, forgive myself, and live a life full of love, joy and peace in the Holy Ghost.

We remember Matthew 6:14-15. "For if you forgive other people when they sin against you, you're heavenly Father will also forgive you.

In Galatians 6:7, we read. "Be not deceived; God is not mocked: for whatsoever a man soweth, that shall he also reap. -KJV

Proverbs 25:21-22 also makes a recommendation: "If your enemy is hungry, give him food to eat; if he is thirsty, give him water to drink. [22]

And finally, John 10:10 states, "The thief comes only to steal and kill and destroy. I came that they may have life and have it abundantly. -KJV

Chapter 7

MIND RESET

The mind is defined by Merriam-Webster dictionary as "element in an individual that feels, perceives, thinks, wills, and especially reasons."

Life's biggest FEAR we must conquer is FEAR itself. To be victorious and triumph in all things we must have the mind of Christ to defeat the negative words within ourselves and block the toxic words of others. Often, we are living in a place of bondage without realizing how we are captivated by someone or something. We all need a mind reset. Some need a complete overhaul, while others may need a renewal occasionally. This is especially true with relationships where the initial focus and reason for being in the relationship can wither after a period of time, and couples either agree to part ways, attend counseling, or renew their vows.

We all have areas of our lives where we are stronger in some and weaker in others. For the stronger areas, we need a renewal and for the weaker areas, we need a mind reset. There are so many thoughts that cross our minds we don't act upon or utter the words we want to say. We are mindful of other's feelings and watch our tongues that keep us out of trouble. We constantly must be mindful of the thoughts we are thinking and what we speak and act upon with those thoughts. Acted-upon-thoughts can position you in a place of opportunity or opposition. We live in a politically correct society where offending people is considered inappropriate, however it depends on the culture or religious views to determine an interpretation of what is correct. Your background and beliefs play a great part in how others perceive or receive your words and actions. What may be offensive to one person may not be offensive to another. If at all possible, we need to be careful with how we present our thoughts to others, as not everyone may not receive them with joy and enthusiasm.

Thoughts roam in our minds regarding subjects of: paying bills, our kids' safety, college costs, loan debts, health concerns, bad relationships, stress, pressures on the job, business failures, car troubles, house repairs and accomplishing our dreams. As Christians we are told by God not to worry. If you are in a committed relationship with the Lord (and a relationship entails spending time in worship, prayer, studying his word, giving financially, serving others, and having His character) then we must give ALL of our cares to him. The Bible says if you love the Lord, you will keep his commandments. Trusting people can be challenging but God wants us to trust him. Why do we worry? It's at this point we need a mind reset. If Christ has become secondary to these common worries, we must be reminded of who God is and how awesome He has been in the past. God always has a process of trust He takes us through. It's not always going to be easy. What doesn't hurt you makes you stronger. I recommend reading Dr. Caroline Leaf's books on the mind/brain connection and how your thoughts set your life up for success or failure.

Here are some reversal confessions you can speak to yourself:

Old Mind	Renewed Mind
I'm ugly	I'm fearfully and wonderfully made.
It's hopeless	I can do all things through Christ who strengthens me.
I give up	I press forward toward the mark for the prize of the high calling in Christ Jesus.
I'm lonely	God will never leave me nor forsake me.
I'm broke	I will sow much that I will reap much; I give that it shall be given unto me.
I'm lost	I know the plans he has for me, plans to give me a hope and a future.
I'm stressed	I will cast my cares upon the Lord. He cares for me.

Old Mind	Renewed Mind
	He takes all my yokes and burdens.
I'm sick	By the stripes of Christ Jesus, I AM HEALED.
I'm tired	I will not grow weary in well doing; I will reap if I faint not.

Write down your thoughts where you have been discouraged and have given up, Why?

1)_____

_____

_____

2)_____

_____

_____

3)_____

_____

_____

What kind of support would you need to think positive about your situation?

1)_____

_____

_____

2)_____

_____

_____

3)_____

_____

_____

Who or what is blocking you from moving toward your goals?

1)_____

_____

_____

2)_____

_____

_____

3)_____

_____

_____

We must get support in our process.

   1) Family/Spiritual Advisor/Coach

   2) Pray and Read the Bible

   3) Say something positive everyday

Mind reset renewal strategies are as follows:

   1) Financial trouble: Continue to give to God financially and he will open up opportunities cancelling the works of the enemy for your sake. Pray the Jabez Prayer in the Bible. Look into the gifts and talents you have and see how you can volunteer, serve God, and become employed or an entrepreneur.

   Deuteronomy 8:18: " But remember the LORD your God, for it is He who gives you the ability to produce wealth, and so confirms His covenant, which He swore to your ancestors, as it is today."-NIV

2) Worry: Our heavenly father knows what we have need of. We have to trust God. Part of our mind reset process is to stop worrying.

Read Matthew 6:25-33 "25 "Therefore I tell you, do not worry about your life, what you will eat or drink; or about your body, what you will wear. Is not life more than food, and the body more than clothes? 26 Look at the birds of the air; they do not sow or reap or store away in barns, and yet your heavenly Father feeds them. Are you not much more valuable than they? 27 Can any one of you by worrying add a single hour to your life? 28 "And why do you worry about clothes? See how the flowers of the field grow. They do not labor or spin. 29 Yet I tell you that not even Solomon in all his splendor was dressed like one of these. 30 If that is how God clothes the grass of the field, which is here today and tomorrow is thrown into the fire, will he not much more clothe you—you of little faith? 31 So do not worry, saying, 'What shall we eat?' or 'What shall we drink?' or 'What shall we wear?' 32 For the pagans run after all these things, and your heavenly Father knows that you need them. 33 But seek first his kingdom and his righteousness, and all these things will be given to you as well."

Peter 5:7 says, "Cast all your anxiety on him because he cares for you"-NIV

3) Stop Complaining: Complaining will only exasperate the problem not stop it or make it go away. Pray, seek counsel and ask God for wisdom in the situation. The children of Israel complained about being in the wilderness and those who did never entered into the promise land.

4) Declaration: We must speak things that are lovely, positive, and focus on good things that will happen every day and stop focusing on what is negatively happening. What you think about will grow.

Romans 4:17 states, "As it is written, I have made thee a father of many nations, before him whom he believed, even God, who quickeneth the dead, and calleth those things which be not as though they were." -KJV

Philippians 4: 8 reminds us, "Finally, brothers and sisters, whatever is true, whatever is noble, whatever is right, whatever is pure, whatever is lovely, whatever is admirable--if anything is excellent or praiseworthy--think about such things."-NIV

Romans 12:2 advises, "Do not conform to the pattern of this world, but be transformed by the renewing of your mind. Then you will be able to test and approve what God's will is—His good, pleasing and perfect will. -NIV

Chapter 8

SHARING IS CARING

In society, these days sharing and being considerate of others is common. Yet it is more normal among our associated groups of interest. Ordinarily, we are not willing to give someone our money, talents or time if they are outside of our interests. The 2016 *World Giving Index* shows America as one of the top three highest charitable nations. This is measured by helping a stranger, donating money to a charity, and volunteering time to an organization. *The 2016 Conversation* articles showed a declined with America giving charitable contributions from

66.8% in 2002 to 53.1% in 2016. There are reasons for the decline: economic factors, less interest, other obligations, and a decrease in disaster relief aid. When we give to family, churches, friends and charitable organizations, it takes our minds off of our own problems, and gives us a sense of pride and a good wholesome feeling about helping others. On a national and global level, you can see America has been a strong force when contributing to nations.

What is it about individuals in society that determines who and when we give to others? Giving is not only monetary-related but also includes our time and talent. When it comes to people we love and care about we have no reservation about giving and putting a smile on their face. We will buy them a gift, take them around town, go out to eat, sing, dance, perform, and make them feel comfortable. It's important to realize that when we give to people it may not be the same people we will receive from. We should just naturally give, especially when it comes to services such as feeding/clothing the homeless, meals on wheels, and offering spiritual advice and counsel. Sometimes we will just receive the satisfaction that someone is being blessed.

Sometimes, we all have had the opportunity to give to a stranger, acquaintance, a neighbor, but we hesitated.

Why are we more prone to giving to charity when someone in our personal midst needs help? As children we're trained about "stranger danger" and with people we don't know, we are told to keep our distance. Yes, we need to have wisdom and make sure that we and our loved ones are safe. The Bible teaches us about alms, giving to poor people and that our hearts must be in the right place to give. The world has become a dangerous place and we must be cautious. Pray before giving to make sure no harm will come to you, but don't discount the one who may be right in front of you. Sometimes the people in front of you may not need food or shelter but also words of encouragement, a hug, a smile, a thank you, or a gift. There are so many ways to give.

Some people feel like they should receive when they give to others. If they feel they have not received in a timely fashion, it could deter them from giving again, or create concerns about how much they should give in the future. They have an attitude of "What about me?" "What's in it for me?" "No one ever gives me anything" and "When will someone care about what I need." Of course, I have fallen into one of these phrases and wonder when someone will take the time to see about my needs, wants, and desires. One thing I remember is how the Lord has taken care of me over the years. Being independent of others, I put my dependence on the Lord and he has always made a way of provision. I've served others in the past, and continue to serve and give to the church, the community, and bless people by various means. A famous well-known scripture is that of John 3:16 "For God so loved the world that he gave his one and only Son, that whoever believes in him shall not perish but have eternal life." -NIV

God gave his Son, Jesus Christ, who was perfect for an un-perfect people. Christ was willing to die that we would have direct access to the heavenly father. No man comes to the Father but by Jesus Christ. He is the only way, the truth, and the light.

What are some reasons you have not given?

1)_____

_____

_____

2)_____

_____

_____

3)_____

_____

_____

4)_____

_____

_____

Now write about times that things worked out for you:

1)_____

_____

_____

2)_____

_____

_____

3)_____

_____

_____

4)_____

_____

_____

"Money Crashers" states there are actually benefits of giving
https://www.moneycrashers.com/benefits-charitable-giving-donations/:

Activate the Reward Center in Your Brain

Improve Life Satisfaction

Feel Happier

Protect Your Local Community

Improve Key Measurements of Your Health

Reduce Rates of Stress

Induce Civic Engagement

Improve Your Employee Morale

One thing to do is realize that God is behind the supernatural instances that happen. There may have been times when money showed up in your account, someone bought something for your child, you got extra time to pay a bill, someone gave you money, or took you out to eat. When you add up the positive things that have happened over the years you become thankful and grateful to God for how He sent people to you just when you needed someone. Also realize that there IS someone outside right now that does not have what you have. Someone who has no home, no car, no family, no food, no hygiene, no job, no peace, no loved ones, and the list goes on. When you compare your life to someone else's, you will realize that with what you have, you are still blessed. Try giving and sharing with others. You always have something to give. You'll be glad you did!

Name some ways you can share something or give something to someone this week (remember it does not have to be money), and write down how felt.

1. _____

2. _____

3. _____

4. _____

In 2 Corinthians 9:7, 11, we read, "Each of you should give what you have decided in your heart to give, not reluctantly or under compulsion, for God loves a cheerful giver. "You will be enriched in every way so that you can be generous on every occasion, and through us your generosity will result in thanksgiving to God." -NIV

James 2: 16 states, "If one of you says to them, 'Go in peace; keep warm and well fed,' but does nothing about their physical needs, what good is it?" -NIV

Malachi 3:10 declares, "Bring the whole tithe into the storehouse, that there may be food in my house. 'Test me in this,' says the Lord Almighty, 'and see if I will not throw open the floodgates of heaven and pour out so much blessing that there will not be room enough to store it.'-NIV

Also, in Luke 6:38 we are told, "Give, and it will be given to you. A good measure, pressed down, shaken together and running over, will be poured into your lap. For with the measure you use, it will be measured to you." -NIV

Chapter 9

OVERCOME ALL

*A*n "Overcomer" as defined by dictionary.com is someone who is able "to get the better of in a struggle or conflict, conquer, fear, defeat, to prevail over, surmount, to overpower or overwhelm in body or mind, to overspread or overrun, to gain victory, win, conquer."

Life has presented us with a daily load of challenges. There is not one person that has not encountered challenges on this journey called Life. The challenges will definitely vary depending on your particular situation. It's interesting to note that one's perspective is a determining factor on whether that situation is considered a challenge. One person who loses a job may not consider it a challenge if the job was extra income. If a person loses a job as their main source of income, it would be considered a challenge and he or she will have a financial struggle. In life you may think you are the only one struggling with a particular situation. Christ states you will have trials and tribulations but do not fear, Christ has overcome the world. He has overcome all things and situations we encounter living in this world. Once Christ was resurrected he proved there is nothing earthly with more power than him. Nothing can defeat him regardless of the person, place, or thing. Christ has given us the ability to tread upon our trials and stand tall on top of them, putting them underneath our feet. Don't give your situation more of your time, money, emotions, and energy. You have the power to control your responses with the word of God. Don't let your responses control you.

Some common areas of life we have to overcome:

Financial Struggles: God wants us to be good stewards with the things he gives us. The Bible says if we are faithful in the little things we will be faithful in much. There are some people who earn enough money to cover their expenses and have money left over for extracurricular activities and entertainment. Others earning money may have to make payment arrangements, budget, and perhaps borrow money to keep up with the expenses. They may or may not have any money to save. We have to take an examination of our needs and wants, and see if there are any areas we can possibly downsize or cut back on to maximize our income. It will take discipline and faith in God.

Malachi 3:10-11 says, "Bring ye all the tithes into the storehouse, that there may be meat in mine house, and prove me now herewith, saith the LORD of hosts, if I will not open you the windows of heaven, and pour you out a blessing, that there shall not be room enough to receive it. And I will rebuke the devourer for your sakes, and he shall not destroy the fruits of your ground; neither shall your vine cast her fruit before the time in the field, saith the LORD of hosts."-KJV

We have to trust God that when you give him your portion he will open up opportunities for you to receive employment and favor in other areas. It may not be what you want at that particular time but he will make sure you are not begging others for help. I have seen how my tithe of 10% of my gross income has allowed me to have continual income. The job position may not be my choice; however,

I've never had to beg for anything or live in an uncomfortable situation. As a believer it's part of the covenant of God that the first belongs to him and he will take care of the rest. It's interesting how for some it's difficult to give God at least 10% and we don't even realize that we allow the government to take much more and don't complain about that. To receive the blessings of God, know that he is a God of exchange. If you want from the Lord, first we must give to the Lord.

Singleness/Relationships: Being single and being in a relationship can be a challenge. It's something I have experienced for decades and much longer than my heart's desire. Let's face it, unless you are making an extreme amount of money, most people, partly for financial reasons, desire a spousal companion. With the support of someone, life is easier and the struggle won't be as difficult. We naturally want to ease our situations and not be in a place of heartache, struggle and despair. No one wants to be in an uncomfortable place. The challenge we meet as believers is to realize the uncomfortable place is where we draw closer to Christ, knowing we have to rely on him to guide us and help us. We must know that Christ is the only one who can fulfill our life and provide for our needs.

As it says in Philippians 4:19, "And my God will meet all your needs according to the riches of his glory in Christ Jesus."- NIV

When Jesus called the disciples they left everything and began to live uncomfortable lives traveling with Christ and learning about the Kingdom of God. They were trained and challenged to heal the sick, raise the dead, cast out demons, and walk by faith. Following Christ is a faith walk and trusting the unknown is uncomfortable. However, it is from the viewpoint of the uncomfortable place we get to see God's faithfulness, His gifts, and his love. We also will experience his favor, his glory, His peace, His power, His strength, His mercy, His joy and His presence. There is a peace you will have when you decide to have a relationship with Him. You have to overcome the feelings and fear of struggling and being alone. God says he will never leave you nor forsake you. When worried, pray to God and ask him to help you. Ask him to show you the way. Ask him to be your Father. Ask him to be your provider. Rise above, build yourself in Christ, grow and develop a relationship with him. In doing so, the less you will focus on what you're a missing in a spouse and the more you will focus on him. Tell him you not only need him, but you Love him and thank him for who he is and the great things he has done in your life.

Health Concerns:

The Lord says in Matthew 6:25, "Therefore I say unto you, Take no thought for your life, what ye shall eat, or what ye shall drink; nor yet for your body, what ye shall put on. Is not the life more than meat, and the body than raiment?"-KJV

As Christians our bodies are a temple of the Holy Ghost meaning the Holy Spirit is to have full access to our lives with our thoughts, our heart, our body, and our emotions. The Holy Spirit should guide you in all situations. You must speak positive words over your body. You must forgive people. As mentioned earlier forgiveness is a must for your healing process. You must ask the Lord to breathe his breath of life into you. I can't emphasize how important it is for you to value yourself and love who God made you to be. Often, words that others speak, rejections from jobs and family, bad news, stress, depression, hopelessness will contribute to the degradation of your health. What you think and mediate on, you will become. The Bible says that we are to mediate on his word day and night. The devil's job is to distract you, turn away from God, and not draw to Him.

Speak affirmations like: *I am healed, I am loved, and have a purpose, I am a good person, I have gifts/talents, I love myself, I have something to offer in this world, good things will happen for me, I will not worry, and I trust God's plans for my life.*

I had to constantly speak words of affirmation over my own life. There were only a few people that were Holy Spirit led to pray for me. I began to lay hands on my body due to off and on pains that lasted for a year. I spoke health, forgiveness, good news, God's love, his mercy, his breath of life, his graciousness, his abundance, his purposed life for me, his joy, his peace and I felt better day by day. Doctors are not God and even though they have abilities to help, they don't know everything. God supersedes medical science. Trust in the Lord, Pray, Get Prayer, and speak these scriptures over your life. If you are harming your body with alcohol, drugs, or bad foods, then change your behavior and ask God to cleanse you and believe for your healing. Jesus healed the men with leprosy but he also said, "Go and sin no more"

I Peter 2:24; Psalms 103:3; Psalms 107:20; Exodus 15:26; Jeremiah 30:17; Proverbs 3:7

Overcomers do not let obstacles defeat them. You must conquer and prevail over the situations attempting to keep you in a hopeless place. The enemies around you and the devil himself wants you in a place of anger, bitterness, and living upset. In this manner you have allowed an evil spirit to overpower the Holy Spirit that lies within you. Galatians 5:22-23 talks about the fruit of the spirit and how we should reflect Christ and how we should not reflect Christ. It tells you how to walk in the character of Christ. This is how you will overcome any situation. Revelation 12:11 talks about overcoming the enemy by the blood, the Lamb (Christ), and word of your testimony. Overcoming leads to a testimony giving you power and authority to alleviate the traps of the enemy. Defeat allows the enemy victory. Being an overcomer brings victory through Christ. Push, pray, and prevail; you are on the winning side.

Name some areas in your life you need to overcome:

_____

_____

_____

_____

_____

Name 3 obstacles hindering you from overcoming:

_____

_____

_____

_____

_____

_____

_____

_____

_____

_____

_____

_____

_____

_____

_____

Name 3 people you can call on to hold you accountable weekly.

_____

_____

_____

_____

_____

_____

_____

_____

_____

_____

_____

_____

_____

_____

_____

Chapter 10

SPIRITUAL WALK

C hristian spiritually is defined as allowing the Holy Spirit to have control over our lives, putting aside our own thoughts, actions, desires and submitting them to the Holy Spirit. We want to make sure that we define how spiritual Christianity should be reflected among His people. There are so many people that say, "I am a spiritual person." What that means to one person does not necessarily mean the same thing to another. We have to be aware of what the Bible says "be wise as serpents and innocent as doves." The Bible tells us in 1 John 4:1 "Dear friends, do not believe every spirit, but test the spirits to see whether they are from God, because many false prophets have gone out into the world." -NIV

We have to be careful and not be misled that as Christians we recognize the people we encounter and whether or not they truly represent Christ, son of the living God. There are so many religious groups where the deception of the enemy is set to make you believe that we all serve One God; we just have many different ways of worship or routes to get to God. There is only one way to God and that is through our Lord and Savior Jesus Christ.

John 14:6 says, "Jesus answered, "I am the way and the truth and the life. No one comes to the Father except through me."-NIV

As mentioned earlier the Holy Spirit is a teacher, counselor, and helper. The Holy Spirit is also our advocate who dwells within us, reveals truth, knowledge, wisdom, gives us power and spiritual gifts, prays for us, gives us life, and enables us to bear good fruit.

Here are some scriptures to reference:

John 14:26; John 16; I Corinthians 3:16; I Corinthians 2:10-11; I Corinthians 12: 7-11; Acts 1:8; Ephesians 1:13; Romans 8:26-27; Romans 8:10-11; Galatians 5:22-25

We don't realize that the Holy Spirit is available, willing and ready to help us in any situation. Often, the people in the world will say words like "something told them" or "I felt it in my belly" and maybe it was the Holy Spirit instructing them and giving them an answer in a particular situation. When trying to live by the Spirit, you want to compare your characteristics with the character of the Holy Spirit. If someone's actions, behavior, and lifestyle are contrary then they are serving a different spirit, not the Holy Spirit. This is important to know so we can be careful who we allow to influence us by suggesting the path we should take. It could be an evil spirit leading and directing you astray from the purpose and assignment of the Lord. Stay away from any person leading you astray from the Holy Spirit. Stay on track with the Lord. The Bible says the world is filled with the lust of the flesh, lust of the eyes, and the pride of life. These principles do not align with the Lord and therefore we should not follow after these deceptions of the enemy.

Here are a few comparison examples of the Holy Spirit vs an Evil Spirit

An evil spirit's purpose is the opposite of God, in his reflection, action, declarations, and deeds. An evil spirit is also known as a demon sent from the Devil to cause us to live harmful and unproductive lives. Evil is defined as anything with bad character, bad qualities, is immoral, wicked, corrupt, perverse, wrong, and has evil thoughts, evil deeds, and speaks evil words. It also produces unhappiness, sorrowful distress, misfortune, pain, chaos, and experiences of loss or calamity.

We can read in John 10:10, "[10] The thief comes only to steal and kill and destroy; I have come that they may have life, and have it to the full." -NIV

When we look at the situations in our lives we have to see if the work of the Holy Spirit or an evil spirit is directing our actions. So often we carry out behaviors we think are just human nature not realizing that we are demonstrating a spirit that lies within us good or bad.

Ephesians 6:12 states, "For we wrestle not against flesh and blood, but against principalities, against powers, against the rulers of the darkness of this world, against spiritual wickedness in high places."

-KJV

Often, we have to distinguish and evaluate ourselves on how we are presenting ourselves to mankind. Possibly, the things people say about us that aren't favorable could possibly be true. No one is perfect and we all have sinned. We must strive daily toward the perfection of Christ.

Read Galatians 5:19-21

Take a moment and reflect on what the Holy Spirit looks like versus an Evil Spirit.

Let's ask some questions

What will people say about you at work?

_____

_____

_____

_____

_____

_____

_____

_____

_____

_____

What does your family say about you?

_____

_____

_____

_____

_____

_____

What does your church/clubs/organizations say about you?

_____

_____

_____

_____

_____

_____

Based on your answers, take a few minutes and do a comparative checklist between the Holy Spirit's influence and an Evil Spirit's influence. The Bible says that we are to look and reflect Christ as Christians. If the evil spirit side is greater than the Holy Spirit, this lets you know areas you need to work on, and grow in your spiritual walk.

The process to have a successful spiritual walk:

1. Take the time to recognize areas of improvement.

2. Start with one area of improvement and replace it with one characteristic of the Holy Spirit.

3. Continue each area for 21 days and then switch to another area.

4. Have your accountability partner check in and listen to him or her.

5. Surround yourself with Godly Men and Women with a solid spiritual walk.

We have to be careful of who is speaking and directing our lives.

Psalms 1:1-2 reminds us, "Blessed is the one who does not walk in step with the wicked or stand in the way that sinners take or sit in the company of mockers, ²but whose delight is in the law of the LORD, and who meditates on his law day and night. I Corinthians 15:33 warns us, "Be not deceived: evil communications corrupt good manners." - KJV

We have to be careful who we surround ourselves with during our growing process. Christ only had His disciples to walk with him learning from his teaching day to day. He had them supporting Him in his journey. Your walk should encompass people who will challenge you, encourage you, and support you in your walk with God and in your personal pursuits. Life will be full of trials, disappointments, pains and rejections, however what is important is how you handle those situations. Are you going to allow an evil spirit to come and gain control over that situation or the Holy Spirit? Sometimes we have to just walk away and be alone for a while, to think about the best way to respond.

James 1:19 declares, "My dear brothers and sisters, take note of this: Everyone should be quick to listen, slow to speak and slow to become angry."-NIV

Choose this day to say you want to live a life where people consider you an asset and an example for others. This walk with the Lord is a process and we are to work daily on our salvation (our freedom) in Christ. We can't do it alone, but by prayer, fasting, and reading we can be successful and live our live on purpose making a positive impact in the lives of those we encounter every day.

Chapter 11

UNMET EXPECTATIONS

Who has wanted so much for your life that the thought of not achieving your goals is unimaginable? At times we have goals however the execution of those goals stays on the back burner to avoid defeat and rejection. Others set the bar so high that if their goals are not achieved in a certain period of time, they become frustrated, give up, and move on to the next venture, not realizing that meeting their goals will take time, money and effort. Good things come to those who wait. A person may have goals and because of rejection repeatedly, after a period of time, it's easier to accept life the way it is and settle rather than encounter unmet expectations.

For example, a young man in college has the desire to work in finance as a banker and then eventually become a mortgage broker. He has been studying hard in school, taking the right classes, and previously spoke with his counselor about internship opportunities working over the summer. He eventually receives an opportunity to work as an intern over the summer as a bank teller, and twice a month is granted the opportunity to sit with a mortgage broker on some of the client conversations. He is an overall B+ in student in school. He has classes that are challenging due to his lack of interest but has an A in his finance class. He will be graduating next year. Next year comes and he has graduated with the hope and expectation he will be offered a job at the bank where he has interned for the last 2 summers. Upon speaking with the Branch Manager, he was informed that he had no openings but would keep the recently graduated student on his potential candidate hire list. Meanwhile the student has put out several résumés, professional letters of recommendation, and despite his efforts continues to run into roadblocks.

Upon researching he realized most bank teller positions, including the bank where he interned over the summer have personality quizzes and some prefer you to be bilingual. He becomes discouraged and cannot comprehend why he receives a rejection letter for not meeting the quiz standard and goes to his former branch manager to inquire. Unfortunately, there's a standard to determine how well applicants can work with customers and the formula is unknown. The recently graduated student does not speak another language, and he does not want to leave his hometown in case of missing a job opening at his former bank. Two years go by and he ends up working for a call center in customer service and never received a call from his former bank manager. He put his is goal and desire to be finance teller on the back burner and decided he no longer wanted to work in the banking industry.

What do you do when you have expectations from others but they have not allowed you to excel regardless of your money, effort or time?

_____

_____

_____

_____

Here are some things most people do:

1) Give Up.

2) Put it to the side.

3) Keep trying with minimal enthusiasm.

4) Go back to School.

Too often we talk ourselves out of our own dreams because of other people's criteria and we measure ourselves against their standards and not our own. What happened to that person that was confident and sure that their checklist will be met? So many us have erased our checklist and made new ones based on society's fluctuating standards.

When this happens you do this:

1) Speak and Write your Vision Every day.

In Habakkuk 2:2 we find, "Then the LORD answered me and said: "Write the vision And make *it* plain on tablets, That he may run who reads it." -KJV

2) Evaluate your skills.

Daniel 1:17 stresses, "As for these four young men, God gave them knowledge and skill in all literature and wisdom; and Daniel had understanding in all visions and dreams." -NIV

3) Pray and Ask for God's favor with Him and with others.

Proverbs 3:4 tells us, "Then you will win favor and a good name in the sight of God and man."- NIV

4) Be thankful and serve.

Acts 20:35 reads, "In everything I did, I showed you that by this kind of hard work we must help the weak, remembering the words the Lord Jesus himself said: 'It is more blessed to give than to receive.' "-NIV

5) Start your own business.

Deuteronomy 8:18 encourages us, " But remember the LORD your God, for it is he who gives you the ability to produce wealth, and so confirms his covenant, which he swore to your ancestors, as it is today.-NIV

Too often when we have unmet expectations we blame others for our life. For example: *This didn't happen because he left me; I'm not making enough money because they didn't hire me; I owe taxes because I'm not married and/or have no children; I have health issues because of other people rejecting me and it's stressing me out.*

While these are valid points remember that in Christ we can rise above any and all situations. In order to live a life that is fulfilling and enjoyable we must rise above all situations. No longer can you allow others to determine your value, your worth, and your influence in this world. You were not created to be a copycat and follow the shadow of another person. Its time to create your pathway, tear up those weeds, get the clutter out of your life, find spiritual advisors, and don't let your life go to waste. God purposed and made us all for a reason. There will be challenging times we must go through but with friends, prayer, deliverance, and fasting, you will make it. Don't let defeat become the best of you, rise from the ashes and shake off the dust!

We also have those people who set their expectations very high. Some may call them overachievers but they are really visionaries. Many visionaries go against the grain and the status quo and remain alone or have very few people around them in their pursuits. They should take note to be careful of the naysayers who will try to pull them out of their passion. For example, a young teen girl has the passion to own a business making tailor-made sneakers. Most people may say there are so many sneakers and colorful sneakers it would be better and less demanding to buy what you want and decorate it yourself. The young lady does not have the support of her peers and her family does not have enough money to fund her project and upfront costs. The young lady looked into an entrepreneurial class for teens in her area and with parental permission reached out to a local entrepreneurial group. She joined the group and got information on how to set up a business, and how to research the sneaker industry. Her goal was to have customers purchase her sneakers with the options to choose from such as: custom design, color, quantity, size and exterior object items. It took one year to get her licenses, business cards, and develop business contacts in the sneaker industry. It took her 3 years to finalize her international business dealings and get her sneakers on the market.

Don't let what's uncommon or unpopular deter you from launching your goals and desires. There were many inventors who went outside the box and were determined to launch much of what we own and wear today. You may be the catalyst to start something new and put something original on the market. It will take work and a TEAM to accomplish what God wants you to do. You may start off alone but gradually, God will bless you with people who can SUPPORT you in your vision and help keep naysayers away.

Who has attempted to put your fire out and discourage you? What and Who is holding you back?

_____

_____

_____

_____

_____

_____

_____

_____

_____

_____

_____

_____

_____

_____

Here are some ways you can stay focused:

1) Realize accusations will come.

Revelation 12:10 informs us, "Then I heard a loud voice in heaven say: "Now have come the salvation and the power and the kingdom of our God, and the authority of his Messiah. For the accuser of our brothers and sisters, who accuses them before our God day and night, has been hurled down." -NIV

2) You are a conqueror.

In Romans 8:37, we read, "No, in all these things we are more than conquerors through him who loved us"-NIV

3) Push pass your obstacles

Philippians 3:14 says, " I press toward the mark for the prize of the high calling of God in Christ Jesus" -KJV

4) Watch who you listen to.

Psalm 1:1 "Blessed is the one who does not walk in step with the wicked or stand in the way that sinners take or sit in the company of mockers."-NIV

5) Get mentors that will awaken your vision.

Acts 9:12 also encourages us in the way of miracles! "And in a vision he has seen a man named Ananias coming in and putting *his* hand on him, so that he might receive his sight."-KJV

Chapter 12

THE PRAYER

Lord, thank you for allowing me to share this time with those who read this book.

You are such an awesome God that regardless of what this life may entail, you are great and mighty and worthy to be praised. Words cannot express how you have been a best friend, a listener, a lover, a healer, a provider, a way maker, a helper, a peacemaker, and more than words can express. I will thank you Father, in the good times and in the bad times. I thank you Father, for providing me with income and giving me food to eat and water to drink. I may not have the finances I want or be in a place where finances are no longer a concern, but during my life you have never left or forsaken me. I have never begged for bread and you have never forsaken the righteous. Thank you Father, for opening up opportunities to give my tithe and offering. This money belongs to you first, and as I continue to put you first, you will always open up a door of opportunity for me. When I apply the principles of giving to you first, then you will supply the other things that I need, want, and desire.

I thank you for giving me peace of mind when I am stressed out. I often cry alone and I know that I can come to you as you have been a listening ear. You allowed me to cry on your shoulder when the everyday survival problems of life seem to overwhelm me and I can't solve them anymore. Everywhere I go people are pulling on me asking me to go here, do this, change that, and no one asks me how I'm doing, or if there is anything that they can do to make my life easier. Sometimes I want to ball up in a corner and never come out. But I thank you God that I look unto the hills from where my help comes from. All of my help comes from you. In you I live, move, and have my being. When my back is up against the wall, you — my Lord — are there.

Thank you for telling me you Love me, for wrapping your arms around me and telling me that everything will be ok. You are available when I call and even when I have made mistakes, been upset with you and others, doubted you, turned away from you; you have always been willing to take me back. I know at times I have taken matters into my own hands as if I have some type of control over my life. It doesn't always feel good to do the Christ-like things.

Thank you Lord, for being with me at the times I have felt like a failure, hopeless, confused about my purpose, and even in the midst of confusion, you have already brought words of hope. There have been people you allowed to speak in my life helping me stay focused and optimistic about my future. I know that my life is not in the fullness of your glory. I am called to live a life that is acceptable and pleasing in your sight. God, on days when I feel down, help me to still walk in the character of Christ. Let me find ways to be salt and light to people and become a witness and an example to those hurting. By the strength of the Father, Son and the Holy Spirit, I can walk in victory. People need to know my journey and I am to no longer wait but get connected with Godly people who will help me grow my spiritual gifts that I may be effective for others. I will continue to seek your face, read, fast, worship and serve others. I will not allow situations and circumstances to keep me down. I am a person who walks in power and authority and will not live a life of defeat. I am not a victim but a victor.

Victory Poem

Victory. Who says it doesn't belong to me?

I don't care who you say that I be —

Where were you when heat was scorching?

The wind was beating and the waves were roaring.

You didn't hear me, the cries drenching my eyes every morning.

People turned their backs, fronts and heads away from me

Oh, poor little baby, they say, not even in front of me —

How can people be so cruel not even to say the smallest little thing?

You know, I was thinking about you this week how is everything?

Too consumed, I've been asking, Will things ever really change?

Lord, it's been a dry desert out here, I now command your blessings of rain.

I have been through the fire, storm, sleet, wind and hail,

With Christ I can stand and in this life I travail —

Victory, Victory, Victory, yes now I will shine!

I place all things under my feet and say NOW it's my Time.

MY STORY

There has not been one area discussed in this book I have not experienced and had to overcome. Of course, this is only a synopsis of who I was and who I am now. The mental, emotional, physically and spiritual components of my journey cannot truly be expressed on paper. However, I hope to give you an insight on my joys and pains and pray it will help you in your own journey.

I grew up in a small town in upstate New York with a population of less than 30,000 people. I knew that the town appeared small yet it had everything I needed, family and friends. The elementary school had only two teachers per grade and despite the size of the town it was actually culturally diverse. All I knew was diversity and as children we enjoyed playing with each other for fun and ethnicity was not a factor. Of course, all of us did not get along, but if there was a problem, it was something another child did like kicking, biting or playing double dare games. I was told to stay away from that kid who was a bad influence for everyone he came in contact with. I have some fond vivid memories of riding bikes, going to friends' homes, and running away from dogs. I'm still not fond of dogs unless they are with an owner. I'm ok now but if they're by themselves I turn another way. As I got older the little dogs grabbed my attention because they are so cute. I never had any pets but I would love to get a cat one day. I'm NOT a cat lady but one cat will suffice. I joined the girl scouts in 3rd grade and developed a good relationship with the girls most of us already knew. My best friend was Hispanic. I was shy to get in front of the class and talk as most kids are but I never had any problems with my neighbors or other students. My parents instilled in us the responsibility to do chores and we actually had a garden we drove to and planted fruit and vegetables. Since I was young, I didn't do any gardening. I just played with the insects and ladybugs and would tear them apart out of curiosity. I really didn't have a care in the world. I also had a few stuffed animals, which was normal for that age but were to be influential to me later on in life.

In school I was an average B/C student with issues in reading comprehension. If I was questioned on the summary, my answers were not the correct answers and I couldn't understand why. If the summary was subjective, how could there only be one answer? A few other students and I between the two classes would have to leave our class and go to an ELA specialist. I also received help from an ELA teacher on Saturdays. This went on for about a year or so.

When I was nine-years-old, my parents had an opportunity to transfer their job to Atlanta, GA. I remember they would take separate trips to Georgia to check on the new home and myself and my siblings had a chance to look at the blueprint draft. It was a time of excitement but I knew I would miss my friends, though I was hoping to make new ones. Little did I know that leaving the old and moving into the new would be a traumatic experience. When we moved to Georgia, our neighborhood had a majority of Caucasian residents. The house was big and beautiful and the neighbors were nice. At school I noticed there was a lack of diversity and for the first time at ten-years-old I felt different and was treated differently by my peers. I had a few peers who befriended me but I was used to getting along with everyone, not just a few. My elementary upbringing consisted of playing with the neighbors, doing chores, playing instruments and completing small projects. I had no issues with my identity and relationships with others. My hair, my clothes, my complexion, confidence level, where I lived, my friends, my personality, my skills were never a concern for me nor in the eyes of others.

When I moved to Georgia beginning in 5th grade my confidence and identity became skewed. I went from not knowing what rejection felt like to questioning my identity and self-worth. In the 5th grade a few people accepted me as their peers and in middle school that cycle continued. My peers were not mean but I was never invited to come to any birthday parties or events. I remember a Japanese friend I sat next to on the bus and there was a boy that sat behind me that use to poke and play with my hair. I was very quiet and didn't speak up for myself, so I didn't even have enough courage to tell him to stop. Even though that went on, my Japanese friend would always bring me a cultural gift around holidays. It's like I had a bittersweet experience at the same time and looking back, God sat me next to someone who cared. I collected more stuffed animals during my middle school years, I played the flute and the piano, and did my chores.

Even though we lived in a nice neighborhood there wasn't a culture of children playing or hanging out with each other. We just remained within our homes and families. This left me with no one to spend time with and my stuffed animals became my friends. I actually enjoyed middle school, teenagers were being silly, and I thought it was funny the things that they did. In 8th grade I had the opportunity to have some friends. Being in a majority Caucasian school, there were not many students who were black, Hispanic or Asian. I decided to join a group of black female friends and things were going good for a few months until a boy became involved. Myself and another friend were interested in the same boy and she and the other girls called me on three way and said all these bad things about me. I realized years later that was bullying. Can you believe one of the girls that was her 2nd time repeating that grade and I did some of her homework just to feel accepted? She was the main one that bullied me and that boy I like indirectly told me I was ugly and didn't talk to me for three years. I'm saying this because the way you are today may be directly related to the circumstances of your past good or bad.

I realized a lot more as an adult. I made a vow at that time and said I will (1) never tell a boy I'm interested in him and (2) never be friends with a group of black girls again. The word "relationship" was pretty much non-existent and my area of self-confidence resided in my academics and music. It was during the early 90s when a dark-skinned woman was not considered beautiful. I went from a girl who lived in New York without cares to a girl in Georgia that didn't have friends, didn't like the way she looked, didn't have the best clothes, and questioned her value. I wasn't needed by anyone anymore. I used stuffed animals to make me feel special and loved. I wasn't able to confide or trust anyone with my feelings, so anything I felt, I internalized. This may be minor for most, however certain things happen in our childhood that influence how we develop and who we become as adults. These are just examples of the issues that stood out, that later were translated into my adulthood. Due to others' mistreatment of me, I went from being open and carefree to closed off and mistrustful of people.

My high school image became a big factor in developing friendships. Mind you, the high school I attended had a black population of 100 out of close to 1900 students. The people that I was acquainted with in middle school began to connect with like-minded groups of people. I became an outsider to black people because I couldn't relate to some of their gossip and behavior. I couldn't connect with the girls because in the area where they lived, families had money. I didn't have the money to dress like the other girls. The only thing that kept me going to feel confident in myself was to be strong academically and I was an honor roll student throughout high school and received an acceptance to every college I applied to. At this stage I knew that boys would not be interested in me, so rather than feel sad, I befriended them. In high school I had more male acquaintances than female. Even though I was never popular, my yearbook is filled with lots of praise for how kind, precious, and sweet I was. That was true. I was not confrontational with anyone, not vengeful, rude, disrespectful, or gossipy. Regardless of how I was treated, I remained the same. If my high school peers saw me today, they wouldn't recognize me, as I have become extremely bold and vocal when I need to be. My life circumstance and situations caused me to develop a backbone of defense and survival. Oh, how the tables have turned!

In my college years I lived in a suite dormitory and met a good friend. We went to church together and we worked together. I had my first boyfriend kiss when I was 18 years old. I met him downtown. He was selling AT&T products on the street. He met my roommates and went to church with me every Sunday. Lo and behold, a few months later I found out he skipped town and went back to live in Pittsburgh. I was totally distraught because we were in a relationship and he just skipped town one day and was gone. The 2nd year of school a situation happened with another roommate, and my friend didn't have my back, and that really made me upset. Looking back at when I was nineteen- years-old, I made a terrible mistake because I stayed mad at her for a few years, ignoring her and acting like she didn't exist, even though we still went to the same church, lived, and worked together. It was during this time that on Nov 1st 1998, God anointed my head with oil and I began speaking in tongues in the dorm room.

All I can describe is that my head was extremely hot and I knew it was God anointing me. Little did I know it would be for the protection and challenges that would lie ahead. It wasn't until two years later that I apologized to my roommate, by that point, she was over the matter and living her own life, unconcerned about me. She ended up getting married, having kids, and going on with her life. I say this to say that it's not worth losing a friendship over small matters. I made the mistake and God blessed her with a family and more. I, on the other hand, still don't have those things. You may think that being rude and vengeful is hurting the other person while it may be, but God is rewarding them as well. Be careful! God is watching how you handle people and various situations.

I met a male best friend and this was probably the best time of my life. We did everything together, went to church, worked together, mentored some youth in our neighborhood, lived in the same neighborhood, though we went to rival high schools. Our parents lived literally ten minutes from each other. When I say BEST friend, I really mean we were the BEST of friends and everyone knew it. After about a year and a half or so, he decided to go back to school, and upon doing so, he began to meet other girls and our friendship slowly began to be more distant. We never thought of actually dating one another but at the same time I couldn't see myself with anyone else. He eventually had to leave the apartment complex and upon doing so, we lost touch and communication for some time. I remember he was interested in a young lady at the church and he was so scared to pull me to the side privately and tell me he was dating someone. At that point, I was not bothered but it was cute because we had been so close, it was like he just had to tell me.

It was during this time I received a prophetic word on who my husband was to be and I was so excited. For two and a half years, I hoped and prayed that he would approach me because I was traditional and felt men should approach a woman. I learned now that I am not so much hung up on that tradition because while I was waiting on him, he ended up marrying another woman. I remember when I was told that I fell down and had a panic attack in the church because I waited only for him. I didn't even think about another man and wondered what happened to the prophetic word.

Remember I enjoyed befriending men since high school so not knowing who I could befriend was a challenge for me. It was at this point, without even realizing it, I somehow believed that I could have what other girls had in a man or have an acceptable godly close male friend. It was around my middle 20s that traumatic experiences in my life occurred. Relationships are just one component, I also experienced hardships in jobs, finances, contemplative suicide, and health as well. To fully understand the full scope, I would have to write another book. My mid to late twenties I accepted the male riffraff type and breadcrumbs of whoever acted like they wanted to be my acquaintance. Once a man I worked with and I we were on our way to go out to eat and we got pulled over. I was driving a rental. The officer was questioning my co-worker more than me and it was my first time experiencing racial profiling. My coworker told me he might get arrested because he had a warrant out for child support. He gave me his mom's number and the key to his hotel room because he wanted me to get his belongings. The police handcuffed him, put him in the back of the police car, and they told me to get out of the car. They had a dog running around the car sniffing for drugs. I was embarrassed and freaking out. They gave me a warning and I nicely went to his hotel, got his stuff and brought it back to the house. That took a few hours and I really didn't even know this guy. While he was in jail, we wrote letters and developed a relationship and I got to know his mom pretty good as well. He got out in 6 months and as soon as he came back to Atlanta a few weeks later, he wanted to end our relationship. Go figure! My skin broke out with eczema due to the stress and working at my job. Later on, another guy I met was a con artist and stole my credit card and used it for his personal bank account. It was my fault because the Bible says make no room for the devil and I gave him the key to my apartment just in case he ever wanted to stop by. Also, he had me watching "The Devil's

Advocate" on a PlayStation 3 he bought with my credit card.

Another guy kept asking me to come by his place and I told him no. So, he got tricky and said he was having a housewarming. Well, since I thought I could go out and mingle, I said yes. But when I showed up there was nobody but him and not using any wisdom, I should have left but I didn't. I stayed for about an hour and I was scared that he was going to harm me since he was an athletic trainer. I finally worked up enough strength to run out of there and to my car and drove off. God warned me and showed me a dream there were two serpents coming to attack me but they never did strike against me and I knew it was these last two guys.

I grew closer to God spiritually during this time. I had spiritual mentors who were prophets and I was amazed at how God was moving through them. They were not well-known superstars; they were just your average everyday people who didn't have much in the natural world but spiritually God was using them mightily. It's interesting to know that we should not judge a book by its cover or judge people where they are in life. God uses the least of these to confound the wise. Intrigued by the prophetic a few years later I became involved with the prophetic ministry. I took prophetic training courses and was singing on the praise team.

In 2008 I had the opportunity to move to Houston TX for a work opportunity. My parents helped me move to Houston and I knew no one or anything about the area. It was a blessing God orchestrated for me to live on a good part of town. Houston was a nice place to live and has a great diversity of people, food and culture. It took me about 4 years to settle in a church home, however once I did the church exposed me to prophetic evangelism. It taught me how to evangelize being led by the Holy Spirit, allowing his words to speak into the lives of people we met in the malls, stores, and coffee shops. I also participated in street ministry on Friday nights with YWAM. This, of course, was where people were on the weekends, in the streets at night. We as laborers went out to do street ministry and it opened my eyes to activities of the night, but also how being a light got people delivered as we continued to come back and pray for people. The ministry was not flashy or well-known but they were doing the work of Christ as Christ would, with no fame or notoriety. They had such humility and the passion to see people free and that's all that mattered. I will forever be grateful to have worked with such an awesome group of people.

I eventually met a man around 2012 in a call center where I was looking for a job. Due to some unethical security process, I declined that job. Not that I was wanting to work in a call center anyway. As I was leaving a man met me on the elevator and he stated he worked there and walked me to my car. We exchanged numbers and talked briefly and it turned into a relationship. Mind you, remember that I just settled for the "breadcrumbs". Any past relationship or acquaintance with a man except for my best friend at nineteen really didn't do anything for me. These men all had kids, no place to stay of their own, no car, and never treated me special like taking me shopping or going out to eat. I had never seen a healthy relationship growing up so I didn't have a standard by which to choose. Unfortunately, I had little to no expectations, but just having some type of company was better than nothing. It turns out that he proposed to me in my apartment and hesitantly, I said yes but I did so because I was in my early thirties and as lady now, my biological clock was ticking. And I didn't think I could find anyone better. One day God told me to take a picture of the ring. I said why? But I didn't do it. Two weeks later the ring, a tablet, my glasses, and some of my bracelet jewelry were gone. I asked him and he pawned the ring and tablet. I told him I wanted the tablet back and I never did get it. He later on opened up and told me he had a problem with cocaine and it was generational because his dad struggled with the same thing. I referred him to get some help, but one day I couldn't take it anymore and ended everything. His stuff was already out of my apartment. When I broke up with him, I saw the demon in his eyes because they turned bloodshot red and another time he was upset with me his voice changed to a high pitch demonic sound. I knew something was wrong and when I moved back to Georgia about a year later a prophet told me I had to repent and there was a generational demon in his family.

In 2013, I returned back to Georgia due to my dad being ill. It was stressful to watch and my mom was very supportive of my dad during that time. I had to start all over with finding steady employment since that time. I returned to work at a call center to get some type of income. I worked 10 hours per day and the home environment was stressful as well. I ended up leaving to live with my brother for some time. When my dad passed, I did come back home to support my mom. Over these last six years I have grown spiritually, going through healing and deliverance sessions and prophetic ministry. I also was dancing on the praise dance team which was by the grace of God. I don't dance so it was God anointing me for that particular season to remain free. I took the prophetic training courses, healing and deliverance courses, and joined the teams to be an asset to others. There has been much growth, however I stopped the growth by leaving the teams due to the demand of both. But I did return to the prophetic teams realizing you should not put your gift under a bushel to make others comfortable. Other people will operate in their talents and it's a shame for me to watch and cheer others while I'm not flowing in what God gave me. That is dishonorable and a slap in his face. However, God has been speaking to me to return to the teams. I am one of his mouthpieces and at times he will use people to confirm his word.

I was told by someone that I care too much about what other people think. At a church the Senior Leaders allowed me to grace the pulpit handling the order of service and learning the importance of social communication. I previously was so focused on my relationship with God and serving him alongside serving others that I didn't understand the power of genuine connection. The church is family oriented and am amazed at the interaction among families outside of the traditional Sunday and Wednesday gatherings. They look out for one another, do things together and worship the Lord. It showed me how differently I was raised and what was considered my family norm.

Why should I listen to others that have no thought or interest regarding my overall well-being except to be judgmental and critical without Biblical reference. Time is ticking and there are people willing to encourage and support me in my gifts. 2020 and beyond is a time to surround myself with like-minded people who will build me up, not tear me down. In 2016 I met a significant other during this time and he was incarcerated. He was a big support for me intellectually, emotionally, and spiritually. Of course financially, romantically, socially, and physically there was not much he could do. This relationship was built on the faith of God he would be released from prison so we could enjoy life together. But his parole was repeatedly rejected. Three times in four years took a toll on me, especially after writing letters to the parole board, speaking with the governor's liaison, talking to the warden face to face, and the visits to the prison after a while were not as fun because I would leave the same way I came, that is, without him. I had to rent a car to see him since mine was twenty years old and I did not want to travel with it that far. It was difficult to say to people I'm in a relationship with someone I've never been to the park with, or the movies. I never held hands with him, or went shopping to a store with him. We've never gone out to dinner together, or traveled and experience those activities many couples take for granted every day. Now at forty-years-old it was a hard decision to let go of something that may never be, but it was the *fear* of being alone that made me struggle with the decision to end our relationship.

Over the years I still dealt with rejection from people, not being offered job interviews, feeling confused why I have not met my mate, and I have been "grinding" making a way for myself for decades operating in survival mode. I've had some issues over the last year, but with the prayers of my sisters and brothers and the word of God, I have kept going and not stopped my love for Christ. No. I may not have the spouse, kids, car, house, job, family, or friends that others experience, but God has been my best friend, never leaving me or forsaking me.

I have dealt with biases, sabotage, lived in public housing and have been a victim of car vandalism. I was conned several times. I moved to another state without knowing anyone. I've ridden on public transportation alone. I've been on food stamps and unemployment compensation several times. Up unto these last few years I haven't had close friends to reach out to for help, and I've had health issues, financial struggles, and identity issues. I've lived alone, experienced job loss, and a lack of financial support, as well as the lack of a healthy love life. I've been passed over and disrespected. I've endured long distance relationships, no car, car breakdowns, and maintenance issues. Though I've been independent, I've known loneliness. I've made some bad decisions along the way but Christ and my representation of him, have always been at the forefront of my mind. Manna has been my provision. I thank my mom and siblings for being a support for me in my life. Many others may think I'm crazy to keep living this holy life, but by my faith, I know change is NOW!

Made in the USA
Columbia, SC
10 June 2020